Successful Steps to Maturity

Pastor Bill Ligon Sr.

With John Wesley Ligon

DEDICATION

To the Master, Jesus Christ, who taught
us how to grow up.

CONTENTS

Introduction

By John Wesley Ligon

I had a little walk with Jesus this week. I was given the task of going over *Successful Steps to Maturity* to prepare it for publishing and it became a journey to remember. On the way I was shown why it's so important to be holy as God is holy. What made a difference in my understanding was that Jesus took me through the door of maturity to show me holiness. If we choose God's way of responding in all our daily decisions we discover that He has made us mature, therefore holy. I was able to appreciate holiness in a whole new light and gained a renewed desire to mature in all my ways. Pastor Ligon lays out the four stages of spiritual maturity showing that each stage has its purpose in the life of the believer. The apostle Peter tells us that as a newborn in the Lord we are to desire the milk of the word, thus setting the stage for the Holy Spirit to transform our lives through the wisdom of Jesus Christ and His word. Those who don't pay attention will not be conformed to the image of Christ and many selfish and foolish decisions are sure to follow. Ecclesiastes 10:16 says, "Woe to thee, O land, when thy king is a child, and thy princes eat in the morning!" Immaturity is devastating to its owner, but woe to the people of the land if he is in authority, for calamity will spread even to the far corners of the nation. So let us consider our own lives in order to choose to be holy by heeding the wisdom of God's word concerning maturity.

What you hold in your hand is really not a book, it's a guiding light. God has declared that maturity is a conscious decision to conform, demonstrated by decisions that are based on God's word and wisdom. This gift of understanding maturity is so practical because it truly applies to the welfare of everyone.

PREFACE

If someone were to approach me and ask, "Pastor, what is the most important thing the church is lacking today"? I would have to ponder my answer only momentarily. For, although there are a multitude of problems facing the modern day church, my response to the question would be "Maturity."

Oftentimes when faced with a problem, as individuals or as a church, we respond ineffectively or inappropriately because we have not properly transitioned through the steps of maturity as set forth in the Scriptures to where we respond as spiritual adults rather than immature children. A child responds according to his or her personal wants and needs, whereas a mature adult responds from the perspective of the needs of other people. So, until we have properly transitioned through the steps of maturity, until we have moved from a place where we view situations only from a selfish perspective to where we view them from an unselfish one, focusing on the needs of other people, we are incapable of responding to other people as God would have us to respond.

In the Scriptures, God sets forth four basic steps to maturity: 1) Childhood, 2) Sonship, 3) Husbandship, and 4) Fatherhood. The first step to developing maturity within our Christian life is becoming a child of God. In John 1:12 we read: "But as many as have received Him, to them He gave the right to become children of God even to those who believe in His name, who were born, not of blood nor of the will of the flesh nor of the will of man, but of God." The second step we will look at is sonship. In 1 John 2:13, John writes, "I am writing to you, young men, because you have overcome the evil one." We will discuss what sonship involves. Then we will look at the third step of maturity which we call husbandship, or management. 1 John 2:10 says, "The one who loves his brother abides in the Light and there is no cause for stumbling in him." In husbandship we develop the ability to manage one-on-one relationships. And lastly, we will discuss fatherhood, which is mentioned in 1 John 2:14 "I have written to you, fathers, because you know Him who has been from the beginning."

These are the four steps to maturity. In this book we will look at each critical step and discuss the necessity for each of us, as children of God, to successfully transition through each step, thus allowing our development from self-centeredness into a proper, healthy, and God-centered Christian life.

1

CHILDHOOD

John identifies four levels of Christian maturity. In 1 John 2:12, he says, "I am writing to you, little children, because your sins are forgiven you." So the first level of maturity in the Christian life is becoming a child of God. John 1:12 says, "But as many as have received Him," -----that is, received Jesus-----"to them He gave the right to become children of God, even to those who believe in His name, who were born, not of blood nor of the will of the flesh nor of the will of man, but of God." Some biblical translations say, "He gave the power to become sons of God." Here we have the Greek word, "tekna", which literally means "children", like a toddler or a tiny little baby, one who cannot care for himself but must be cared for under guardianship. The word, power, or "right", is not the word, "dunamin", used in Acts 1:8 from which we get our word "dynamite" or "supernatural power" but it is the word, "exousian", which means "right" in the sense of receiving delegated authority from someone else. So John says, "As many as have received Jesus to them He gave the exousian (the authority) to become little children of God even to those who believe in His name and who were born not of blood or of the will of flesh or the will of man but of God."

That is good news for the entire world because he is saying that God has delegated the right or the authority to every human being to become one of His little children. That means then that the powers of darkness, the powers of Satan cannot prevent one who desires to be born into the family of God, into the kingdom of God, from experiencing that new birth.

Every person is given a measure of faith. Some use it and some abuse it. If we do not use our faith, Jesus called that "no faith", but we have that faith and that ability to respond. A person who has never heard can believe and receive the Lord Jesus Christ and the powers of darkness cannot keep him out of the kingdom of God. God has delegated to each person that right or authority to become a child of God.

Once we become children of God, it is important for us to develop in our childhood. Just as a new born baby has a period of time for care, nourishment and oversight and just as he or she learns to respect and honor parental authority, so God has intended for Christians to be born into the Kingdom of God and live for a season as little children. During this time they learn to respect and honor spiritual authority in their lives.

In 1 Thessalonians 5:23, Paul says, "Now may

the God of peace sanctify you entirely and may your spirit, soul and body be preserved complete without blame at the coming of our Lord Jesus Christ." Why did Paul put them in the order of spirit, soul and body? Why didn't he say body, soul and spirit? He indicated that we are to be born in such a way that we develop in spirit, soul and body. You remember Jesus said in John 3, "Marvel not that you must be born again." He said, "That which is born of the flesh is flesh and that which is born of the Spirit is spirit." You must be born of the Spirit of God. God's plan is that every person who so desires will be born of the Spirit and then they will have a relationship with Him where they can begin to develop and grow and become the people that He wants them to become.

If you attempt to begin with God at the body level, then you are not going to grow the way you are supposed to grow. There are people who are born and raised within the church who attempt to relate to God either at the soulish level or at the body level and they never really grow spiritually. They become adults or even senior adults, but when you attempt to talk to them about their relationship in Jesus Christ, you find that they are not established in the Lord. So there is no authority in their lives. They still do what they want to do independent of the will of God and without the Holy Spirit working in their lives.

God's plan is that we are born as His children and, for a period of time, live in a state to where we can learn to honor and respect authority in our lives.

We submit ourselves to the will of God and respect and honor those around us.

In John 4, Jesus is speaking with the Samaritan woman at the well. When He begins talking to her about worship, He says that the Heavenly Father looks for those who will worship Him in their spirit. God is looking for people who will have such a relationship with Him that they can commune with Him out of their spirit, out of their innermost being. When they do, they begin to develop a wholesome relationship with God and with those around them.

That is why we are reminded of John 1:12: "As many as have received Him, to them He gave the right or the authority to become little children of God." It is out of that relationship that we begin to develop as healthy, mature, christian people. We must exercise the right to develop our childhood and when we do, God will honor it.

You need to ensure that when you are in a position as a child of God that you are accountable to other people for your life and for your behavior. I frequently meet with a group of men-----the elders of the church-----for accountability and they are allowed to challenge me and acknowledge either my growth or lack of growth, in my relationship with the Lord. They have that access and that privilege to call me into accountability. We do that with each other within the body. Members have the right as members of this church to say, "Pastor, where are you in the Lord?"

In Matthew 18:3, Jesus said that it is absolutely

necessary that you begin at your childhood level in your Christian walk. He said, "Truly I say to you, unless you are converted or changed within and become like little children, you shall not enter the kingdom of God." One of the serious problems that we have in the church today is that there are people who have come into the church and have not matured in their childhood with the Lord. They have not learned how to come under authority. They have not learned how to respect authority in their lives and when they try to function as sons of God, they act like children. They try to function in a partnership with God, only to discover that the rebellion within them that has never been dealt with causes problems in their relationships with other people.

Oftentimes people have come into the church relating at an improper level, perhaps a soulish level, instead of a level of maturity with the Lord. For instance, there are people who go to a particular church because they like the preacher or because they like one of the teachers in the bible training program of the Sunday school. Or, perhaps they might go to a particular church because they want to establish certain contacts with people in that church and have friendships with those people. But then what happens when the person that they are admiring and following does something that disappoints the follower? At that point their faith relationship is destroyed and sometimes people even drop out of church because they have not established their relationship to God at the level of the Spirit. They have not developed themselves within as children of God and are not learning to operate under the authority of the Lord.

Many relationships begin at the wrong level, producing the same destructive results in the lives of the people. There are those even who come to the place that they have learned the right lingo in the church. They can say, "Praise the Lord" at the right time; they can say, "Hallelujah" at the right time; they can carry on all of the externals thereby causing the average person to think that they are spiritual, but in reality they have not developed that inner relationship to the Lord and have moved out of childhood without being established in their faith with the Lord Himself.

A healthy divine relationship with God must develop first in the spirit of the individual. The Bible calls this your childhood. Galatians 4:4 tells us the state of a person who is in his childhood in the Lord. It reads, "Now I say as long as the heir is a child or a little baby, he does not differ at all from a slave, although he is owner of everything." We see in this that when you become a child of God, you enter into the inheritance of everything that God has given to all of us as children in Christ Jesus. It is there and available to you. You become a joint heir with Christ and everything that belongs to Jesus belongs to you. But as long as you are in your childhood, you are put under guardians. Paul says, "Now that guardianship is not unhealthy." It is healthy for us. Once this guardianship and management over our lives has been established to where we come into maturity, then the Lord through the Holy Spirit causes us to begin to cry out, "Abba Father!" We are adopted as sons and because you are sons, verse 6, God sends forth the Spirit of His son into your heart crying, "Abba Father!" or "Daddy!" In other words, the Holy Spirit brings us to the place where we are moved in the power of the Holy Spirit from our childhood into our sonship. This is what he is making reference to here. "Because you are sons, He sent forth His Son and the Spirit of His Son into your heart crying Abba Father. Therefore you are no longer a slave but a son and if a son then an heir through God."

In our childhood we are indeed slaves to our circumstances. A child is a self-centered individual. What is the first thing that a child begins to identify with in life? He finds his fingers and toes and then maybe his nose. He gets to know himself and that is true also in the Christian faith. There are those who are born again. They are children of God, finding their fingers and toes, but they never grow out of their childhood. So the totality of their relationship within the body of Christ consists of them asking, "What is God doing for me? What is in it for me?" They are constantly working to discover their own identity within the body of Christ. "Who am I and what does God do for me?"

It is interesting that when you are in your childhood, God answers your prayers much faster.

Did you ever notice that shortly after you were born again and baptized in the Holy Spirit, almost everything you asked for God gave to you? Then the time came when God shut off the blessings. And you said, "What has happened? Why is God not moving any more in my life?" Well, God is moving but now the Holy Spirit is working on you, bringing you out of childhood and into sonship and finally, into husbandship, so that you can begin developing in a more mature way. If you never move away from "me", "what's in it for me?", then you are not going to grow the way God wants you to grow.

Sometimes people are afraid of stepping out of their childhood and moving into their sonship in Christ Jesus. They are afraid of taking on that responsibility and so go to great lengths trying to make sure that they stay in that comfort zone where God can just take care of them and they do not have to take on the responsibility of other people.

What happens when we attempt to move out prematurely before we have developed our childhood the way we should? Luke 15:11 says, "A certain man had two sons and the younger of them said to his father, give me the share of the estate that falls to me. And the father divided his wealth between them and not many days later, the younger son gathered everything together and went on a journey into a distant country and there he squandered the estate with loose living." In that behavior, the son showed that he was not prepared to manage his inheritance.

Why was he not prepared? Because he did not make the transition from childhood to sonship. If he had made the transition emotionally and spiritually from childhood to sonship, then when it was time for him to go out as a husband or a manager of life, he could have managed his affairs. But he did not make that transition. In doing so, he skipped sonship and tried to become a manager. He did not learn maturity or see the wisdom of maturity but instead, jumped over sonship and as a result failed. It goes back to the proper order of development that needs to take place. The Holy Spirit uses God's word to develop our spirit, in turn bringing peace and wisdom to our soul, and as a result our maturity keeps pace or goes before the natural development of our body. Submission and obedience to God's commandments is where God has placed blessing, wisdom, and development (maturity). A listening ear begins in childhood resulting in wisdom and emotional stability. The peace of God is present in willful submission to God's commandments. As God brings us into spiritual maturity He also brings us into spiritual authority. All the ingredients for maturity are then present and at work.

Sonship is a state where you move out of your self-centeredness into a God-centered lifestyle in which you move away from being positioned before God as Father, saying, "I need this today, give me, give me," to where you take up a position beside the Father and begin looking at life from the Father's perspective and as a partner with God.

A child is a slave.

A son is a partner.

A husband is a manager.

A father is an overseer.

So you see the prodigal son had one serious problem that he failed to recognize. He thought that all he needed was money and that money was going to take care of his needs. But he discovered that money soon disappears and once his money was gone, he did not have the maturity within himself to establish himself in management. Inevitably he came to the place where he was once again enslaved to his circumstances. He had never really stepped out and taken spiritual responsibility; he never made passage into his sonship. He thought that he was free because he had money. Once his money was gone, he realized that he was not at all free. Here he was, a Jewish boy now feeding pigs in another man's farm, in a gentile's pigpen, a slave to an unbeliever. Then it began to dawn on him that there were some things that he had failed to do in his life. He realized that he had failed to recognize the need to transition in maturity from his childhood to his sonship. Back home he never did make the transition and therefore never became a son of his father. He was always a child, not a son. He never learned to be responsible.

In Luke chapter 15 we read that the son came to his senses and decided to go back home, and so he did. He walked into his father's house and repented.

He wisely confessed his sin against God first, thereby declaring his need and desire to come under spiritual authority through obedience to God's commands. Then he confessed his sin against his father, thereby establishing honor in his own heart once again towards his father. He then requested of his father that he make him his slave; his hired servant. What was he saying in this? He was saying that he had never made the transition from childhood to sonship and that he had come back to establish himself in his childhood with the father. He could honor authority, submit himself to authority and prepare to make the transition from being under authority to being beside his father in authority where he would become his father's partner. When he asked to be made as one of his father's servants he was expressing the humility and submission necessary to develop true maturity.

Oftentimes we look at our lives and try to determine why things are failing around us, why the things we put our hands to never succeed, why our relationships fail. Why is it that marriages are failing at a high rate today? Out of every couple who marry, over half of them will be divorced after a short period of time. Why is this so? Why are people failing to manage the affairs of life? The answer goes back to the fact that they are still relating in life as children, in childish ways. A child discovers himself first. Once he discovers himself then he has to discover the world of his father. The world of his father is not just the child's world. It is a world of responsibility, a world of action and integrity. It is a world where you become more concerned with the needs of others.

That is what the prodigal did when he came home and apparently was successful at it. Because the father recognized that the son had come to a place of revelation and enlightenment, he was able to invest in him again. The question is this: Where did the father get the resources to again invest in his son with more inheritance since the father had already given the son his portion? It was reserved in the firstborn blessing. The firstborn blessing is a double portion blessing. When the younger son came back, the older brother had reason to be concerned because he was holding the firstborn blessing and so it was out of those resources that were reserved for the firstborn that the father was able to again establish this son.

The same thing is true with us. We enter into our rebellion and finally come to the place where we reach the end of our rope, the end of ourselves, and come to our senses. One translation says that the prodigal "came to himself." When he dropped down to the bare necessities and with nothing left, he had an epiphany. He discovered his true self, a child; immature in his ways and one who had never learned to respect and honor authority in his life. That is why he went home. When we do this with God, we come to Him and say that we are not worthy to be called His sons but, "Make me one of your hired servants." When we submit ourselves to God, we are born again. In that new birth, God has to give us a new inheritance, we have already blown our first inheritance. Where does He get this new inheritance? He reaches into the life of his firstborn son, the Lord Jesus Christ and takes the firstborn blessing from Him and gives it to us. In the exchange, God puts our sins on Jesus. And that is what it means to be born again. Now we start over. One of the joyful thoughts about this new birth is that God has made provision for a new beginning.

There are many people who have failed in their efforts to manage life. They come into physical adulthood without being established in spiritual adulthood. The answer is to go to Father God admitting failure, asking to come under authority to learn the Father's ways. "I appeal to you, just make me as one of your hired servants," we cry to the Father. And then He gives us the chance to be born again and to start all over. That is what the new birth is all about. It is coming to the place where we are born again and we begin to be established in a right relationship with Father God. We learn to be sons of God.

If as adults or as young people we are having trouble with authority in our lives, we need to examine our own hearts and ask ourselves this question: "Have I been born again?" If the answer to our question is "no", then we understand why we are having trouble with authority in our lives, why we are rebelling, and why our actions are not producing positive results for us. If we determine that we are born again then we can understand that our problem is that we leaped over our sonship and attempted to go directly into the management of life as little children. We behave like little children when we come into relationships with other people; selfish, self-centered, angry, and rebellious. And when we are called on to give account for our actions in the presence of other people we are not able to manage it because we always relate to those threatening circumstances like little children.

When I was a boy playing ball with my neighborhood friends, one boy who owned the ball would sometimes pick up his ball and go home when the game did not go his way. There are a lot of people like that within the church. They either want to play church their way or they take the ball and go home. At times they won't attend to or participate in any ministry of the church because they have never really transitioned out of their childhood into sonship. They had never learned to work under authority.

When you are a little child, God often answers prayers quickly because God has given people the right to experience a childhood for a season. Nevertheless, He will not allow you to remain a child forever. He will bring you to the place where He will challenge your self-centeredness. When you are being challenged, you have to make a decision. You will either rebel against the authority of the Holy Spirit in your life, thereby rejecting the leadership of Father God or you will submit to the authority of the Holy

Spirit in your life. If you rebel you will continually move from one experience to another where you attempt to manage life only to fall into conflict and failure. When you finally realize that the root of your problem is failure to make passage out of childhood-----like the prodigal-----you can come back to Father God submitting to Him, saying, "Father, I want to come back into your house and learn to submit. I want to learn to come under your authority." When you do, the Holy Spirit will teach you to behave as a son and not as a child.

When a person makes transition from childhood to sonship, that person moves into a new area to where he or she begins to experience the power of God in life. There the person develops a concern for others. A child does not minister to other people because he is always relating to life on the basis of personal needs. And we as immature children are not even sure if we can ever respond to life like Jesus. When we come to the place where we begin to move out of our self-centeredness into where Jesus is, we start looking to see how He acts and then we start acting as He acts because we are like Him. We discover several things: First, we discover that Father God does delegate authority. Secondly, we discover that His resources are unlimited. As a child, we are always looking to see what Father is going to give to us. But as a son, we come to the place where we discover that we have the keys to Father's storehouse and that is what the firstborn son in the prodigal story discovered. When he complained to his father that he had always been a faithful son, the father said to him, "Son, you have always been with me and everything I have is yours," and that is also true with us. When we come into sonship we relate to Father God on the basis of what other people need and not on the basis of our own personal needs. We discover that Father God supplies our need, so that we can supply the needs of other people.

That does not happen in childhood. That only happens in sonship. In sonship, Father supplies our needs so we can supply the needs of other people. This is what Paul is referring to when he writes that God supplies all our needs according to His riches in glory and that He abundantly supplies so that we can minister to other people. It is those people who have come to the place of sonship and are concerned about the needs of other people who discover how to let God work through them to help others. A child never gets to know the resources of God. Young christians have many of their prayers answered for a season. Many of their prayers are answered much faster than those of people who are supposed to be mature christians. If they are not careful, seasoned christians will get jealous of the young christians because the young christians get so excited about the Lord and tell about what God has done for them. Then the mature christian may say, "God, I have served you all of these years but You haven't done those things for me." And Father is going to say to you, "Oh my son, don't you know that you are always with me and everything I have is yours." If the firstborn son had wanted a party, he had the authority as a son to say to all the servants, "Go, kill the fatted calf and invite all the friends. I am going to have a party." He could have thrown the biggest party of all.

This is true with us also. Jesus said in his own sonship, "I came as one who serves you." So Jesus offered Himself as a servant and came to give His inheritance away. That is what the cross means. He laid down His life. He died so that others might live.

When we decide that we are going to break out of our childhood, we do so by beginning to give, not receive. We come to the place where we say, "Father God, I am going to stop relating to you on the basis of what I can receive. I am going to begin to relate to you on what I can give." And we discover that there are greater resources in giving than in receiving. While we are learning to give away, after deciding to make the transition out of our childhood and into our sonship, we need to be careful not to judge new christians, young in faith, who only pray to receive blessings. John said in John 1:12 that the new child of God has that right. He has the right to be a child for a season, and so is not judged, just as we do not judge one of our little children at home who is looking to us on the basis of receiving, not giving.

Sometimes I keep chewing gum or candy in my pocket for the little ones at church when they ask for it. Then the next Sunday that child comes running hoping to get candy. When he asks, I give it to him because he is a child. When he becomes a son he will give to others.

We don't judge little children when they come to us for what they can get. We don't judge our young brothers and sisters in the Lord when they relate to Father on the basis of what they can get. But we help them to come to the place where they say, "Lord, it is time for me to step out and begin to give." So they start moving in the direction of giving to other people. When they do, they discover that it is more blessed to give than to receive. The greater blessings come in giving. They thought when they were children that they had the greater blessing by receiving. But now they have decided to make that break and to step out and give. They begin to discover that Father says, "Here I have a partner, I have a son, I have a daughter." They are now giving. And He commands the angels to put more into their storehouses. They need more because they are giving." So they begin to give and soon they discover as partners with Father that indeed there are greater resources in giving than in receiving. They now have moved out of childhood into sonship. They are not ready for management, yet. They are just beginning to discover that it is great to give. So they start giving away and as they do, God begins to put back into their storehouse the supplies needed for ministry to others.

Isn't that true in life? I am not just talking about

money. Let's say today, as a son of God, that you don't feel loved. As one of God's sons, how are you going to begin to experience more love? You find someone to love. Just go out and start loving other people. Start blessing them.

Friendship is another area where a child can develop. You don't feel like you have any friends. Then go out and begin to minister friendship and concern to other people.

Patience is a place of learning. There are two ways to get patience. One is to act like a child and suffer your tribulation repeatedly because the Lord will begin to work in your childhood to teach you patience. Eventually, you will come to the place where you say, "God, you used to answer all of my prayers but You don't answer them anymore and all I get is trouble." However, the sooner you begin to say, "Wait a minute, I am going to accept this with patience," and you begin to rejoice in the Lord. The Holy Spirit brings you out of your childhood into your sonship. You find that patience does its perfect work. The mature handling of the experience brings you to that place. God is not going to leave you in your childhood. Likewise, the time will come when He will begin moving you out of your sonship into your husbandship and into your relationship with other people. How is He going to do that? He will probably put you in relationship with someone that you don't like. He will say to you to team up with that person and work together. Then you will find out who you really are.

God has given you the right to have a healthy childhood. If you have not had a healthy childhood in the Lord, then you have to go back and have it established. If you haven't had a healthy childhood in the natural due to rebellion against authority, you have to come back and say to Father God, "I am a rebel. I have disrespected authority and now I ask you to take me as your child." At that point you can be born again, receive Christ in your life, and submit for the first time in your life to authority.

Did you know that is what being born again means? It means you submit to the Lordship of Jesus Christ. If you are not submitted to the Lordship of Jesus, if you haven't given Him the right to tell you what to do by the Holy Spirit, you need to question whether you have ever been born again? Because being born again means that you come under the authority of Father God. You become His and now He has the right to guide your life and tell you what to do. When you come under His authority and say, "Father, I submit to you, my Lord and my God, please take my life and guide it," then the Holy Spirit is going to begin to nurture you. At first, almost everything you ask for the Father will give you.

I remember when I had my little boys and they couldn't even walk. All they had to do was whimper and I would ask what they needed. I was a servant to them. They would make a funny face and I would change their diaper. Then they would lie back and coo. Then the time came when I said, "Ok young man, you need to feed yourself. Take care of your own hygiene. You are big enough to take care of yourself." Father God is going to do that with us too. We can scream and carry on and be angry at God because He is not still pampering us and treating us like babies, but God is saying that it is time for us to get up and take care of ourselves and other people.

If you haven't come to the place where you can say, "Jesus is Lord over my life, everything about me; my life, my time, my attitude, my relationships," then He is not Lord. And you need to be born again and become a child of God. Why? Because you have that right to become a child of God. If you don't become a child of God and you move out in the world without Him, you are going to find you are not equipped to handle what this world has in store for you. Only in Christ Jesus will you be equipped with the power and authority to succeed as you live submitted to His authority.

Sin outside of Christ Jesus will destroy the strongest rebel. There is no person strong enough to overcome what sin can do independent of Jesus Christ as Lord. It is wonderful to know that we have the right to be children of God. We have the right to come into the Kingdom of God, be born again, have the Holy Spirit nurture us as children and move us into our sonship with its responsibilities.

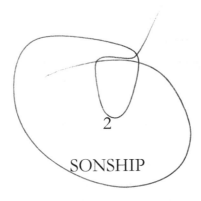

2

SONSHIP

The second level in the steps to maturity is sonship. Sonship is important in our preparation and growth as children of God. It prepares us for the ministry that God has for us. The level of responsibility in society today has grown so weak that it is difficult for people to understand that God is the one who planned life so that we would have four stages of growth.

1) childhood
2) sonship
3) husbandship
4) fatherhood

In this day and age a teenager would not know what "shift for himself" means. Running through the gears of a hot sports car would probably come to mind and put a smile on his face. To tell the truth, it would me too; but, we are so affluent and have so much already in our lives that we don't understand that "shift for yourself" means taking personal responsibility in life.

1 John 2:10-14 says, "The one who loves his brother abides in the Light and there is no cause for stumbling in him but the one who hates his brother is in the darkness and walks in the darkness and does not know where he is going because the darkness has blinded his eyes. I am writing to you, little children, because your sins are forgiven you for his name's sake. I am writing to you, fathers, because you know Him who has been from the beginning. I am writing to you, young men, because you have overcome the evil one. I have written to you, children, because you know the father. I have written to you, fathers, because you know him who has been from the beginning. I have written to you, young men, because you are strong and the word of God abides in you, and you have overcome the evil one." In this passage John identifies four levels of spiritual growth. The first is that of "little children". The word that is used for children is the word teknia. In the Greek it means "little children", ones who cannot assume responsibility for themselves. A child is a slave to his circumstances, bound up by his various circumstances, always relating on the basis of his own emotions and feelings. Then there are "sons".

A son is a junior partner with his father. He comes alongside him and begins to model himself after his father by taking his father's characteristics. That is sonship. The son begins to enjoy some of the authority that his father begins to delegate to him. Then John identifies "husbands" in verse 10. "The one who loves his brother abides in the light and there is no cause for stumbling in him." A husband is one who is able to manage one-on-one relationships with other people just as a natural husband marries his wife and proves that he can manage his household. So in the kingdom of God, a husband is one who enters into a relationship with the Spirit of the Lord and a "koinonia" with others. He relates to others based on his born again relationship with Christ and the fruit of the Holy Spirit. He begins to share in Godly love and service to the life and vitality of those relationships. Lastly, there is "fatherhood", which is an overseer. Fatherhood is one who defines patterns for living and is also one after which others may model themselves in life.

Where is God going with all this? He is taking His children to the place where they and each successive generation can grow spiritually so they can reach their full potential in Christ Jesus and accomplish the Father's will. God wants them to experience life and life more abundantly.

There are many believers who have never broken out of childhood. You may ask, "Pastor, how do you know that?" I know it when they face circumstances that are challenging to them and they react in a childish manner. When we react in childish ways, we are revealing that we indeed have not broken out of our childhood.

God's plan is that we are born again, born as children of God, and embrace our right as stated in

John 1:12: "We have the right to become children of God." For a season of time God wants us to enjoy our childhood but then we need to move on to where we no longer relate the total experience of life to our selfish needs. Instead we begin relating on a basis of what Father sees in the needs of other people.

An English teacher once told her college students how to expand their vocabulary. She said, "If you make use of the same word at least ten times, it will become yours forever." Some of her students began to deliberate upon this nugget of wisdom, wondering if they could indeed increase their vocabulary and expand their horizons by simply using a word ten times. To the students this theory seemed simplistic. But then, in back of the classroom, the faint whisper of a voice came from a coed. She was heard saying, "Bob, Bob, Bob, Bob, Bob, Bob, Bob, Bob, Bob, Bob, he'll be mine forever." She had not broken out of her childhood. She had not come to a place where she understood that there is something greater than meeting your own personal needs in life. We are to take on sonship by relating to life as father relates to life.

In Proverbs 10:1, we find the following: "A wise son makes a father glad but a foolish son is a grief to his mother." The challenge that we all face is that of following God's directions so that we can make the transition from childhood into sonship and begin to take on the characteristics of our father.

There are three goals that are set before us

scripturally as we seek to move into sonship. The first goal is establishing a pattern of fatherhood in our own lives so that we begin looking and acting like the One who is greater than we. We purpose to take on His characteristics in full confidence that He is present within us to fulfill that purpose. The second goal is to develop faith for living because the just live by faith. The third goal is to establish faithfulness for ministry. So the first goal is establishing the pattern of fatherhood. The second is beginning to exercise your faith and the third is becoming faithful in all of your activities for living.

In I Corinthians 13:11, Paul said, "When I was a child, I understood as a child, I acted like a child, I thought like a child, but when I became a man, I put away childish things." That is what God is after in our spiritual growth; to come to the place where we lay aside childish things and take on the characteristics He demonstrates in Jesus.

It is good that the Apostle Paul was able to make that transition. Many times he was in a place in his life where he had to make decision after decision in order to go on with the mission that God had put before him. He faced every possible opposition in life, from stoning, being left for dead, beatings, scourging, threatening, and imprisonments, but it did not deter Paul. He had become a man and put away childish things. He was now moving according to the plan of Father God, not according to his own personal desires.

When life becomes difficult, a child seeks the place of least resistance, moves into a comfort zone where he can feel comfortable and protected in life. A son is one who continually refers to the Father and says, "Father God, what are we going to do in this situation." 1 Peter 2:23 says that Jesus, as the son of God, continually entrusted Himself to God and did not react to His circumstances but yielded Himself to Father God. That is the pattern that God has given us. It is attainable by everyone because of Jesus Christ and what He has done in our lives. He paid the price of sin that He might reside in us through the Holy Spirit. He is in us and now we can successfully do what we cannot do in our own strength.

In Galatians 4:1, Paul talking about the difference between childhood and sonship, says, "I say, as long as the heir is a child, he does not differ at all from a slave, although he is owner of everything. But he is under guardians and managers until the date set by the father. So also we, while we were children, were held in bondage under the elementary things of the world but when the fullness of time came, God sent forth His son, born of a woman, born under the Law in order that He might redeem those who were under the Law that we might receive the adoption as sons. Because you are sons, God has sent forth the Spirit of His Son into our hearts, crying, Abba Father! Therefore you are no longer a slave, but a son; and if a son then an heir through God."

Paul lets us know that the Holy Spirit is given to

bring us out of our childhood into our sonship where we can begin to receive our inheritance in Christ Jesus. It is here that these patterns are defined in our life. The patterns that are established are built around submission to the authority of Father God. God's intention is that submission begins in a healthy home with a healthy mother and father who fear and love God and who guide the children in the right direction. Unfortunately, many people today have been raised in circumstances that are foreign to that lifestyle. So God has made provision for those who have not had the opportunity to be born, groomed, and guided in a godly Christian home where love is present. It is that they begin all over within the context of being born again and being discipled. He is the God of the second chance.

So we are given a new opportunity by being born again as children of God. First we were born as children of our parents but we are born now as children of God. For a season, God gives us the opportunity to ask for almost anything we want. But the day will come when the Holy Spirit will begin working in us, causing us to cry out, Abba Father! In that state He begins to move us out of our childhood and into our sonship. In our sonship, He calls us to begin giving away instead of receiving. We start giving. We start ministering to other people. If, in the Holy Spirit, we make the transition into our sonship and begin ministering to others and learn to give, then the Holy Spirit brings us into our husbandship.

If we do not make that transition, even if we grow up physically in life without being able to make the transition in the Spirit, some unusual things begin to happen in our lives. For instance, a young man who never makes the transition through sonship into husbandship but always stays in his childhood, emotionally and spiritually, will have that inexplicable need within him to have a right relationship with father and to please him.

Many times these young men are vulnerable and get caught in relationships where they are trying to get close to another male, but become enticed and get caught up into homosexual activities. There is not a single place in the Bible where a male is called a homosexual. Translations are given of homosexuality but the word is "sodomy". The word sodomy comes from an experience that happened in the cities of Sodom and Gomorrah where Lot chose to settle in that land and God eventually destroyed the land because men sought physical relationships with other men instead of having healthy family lives. Spiritual immaturity had become so prevalent in society that the citizens of Sodom abandoned the fear of God and all of His moral guidelines. On one occasion angels came to visit with Lot and the word went out into Sodom and Gomorrah that those men had arrived. The men of the city showed up at the door of Lot, demanding that the men, the angels, be sent out so that the men of the city could have sexual relations with them.

What kind of need is this in man? It is the need of a man to be loved by another man. It is a legitimate need in life but it is not legitimate when two men begin to stimulate each other physically. It is legitimate when a mother takes a little daughter in her arms and loves her and guides her and teaches her the ways of the Lord. It is legitimate when a father takes a little girl in his arms and begins to teach her respect and understanding. That father is taking his little girl in his arms to let her know that she can trust manhood; that she does not have to give anything in order to receive love, and so she learns that she does not have to earn that love by giving something physical. She can get close to daddy and daddy is going to honor her and respect her as a handmaiden of the Lord. It is legitimate when a father takes his little son in his arms and affirms him with his love.

However, when all of that becomes twisted and distorted, we get into all sorts of harmful, enslaving activities that woefully miss the plan of God for human life. Fathers demonstrate that they cannot, in a healthy way, get close to their daughters without doing things they shouldn't do. There are situations now where mothers are demonstrating that they are unable to get close to their little boys. There are known cases where mothers have taken baby boys in the crib and physically stimulated them in a sexual way. This is all a result of the failure of our society to make the transition from childhood to sonship in Jesus Christ. Whoever will, though, will assume their place beside Father God and take on healthy relationships with those around them.

In the past, after teaching about these unhealthy sexual problems within society, I have had young men gather around me and say, "You mean to tell me that these feelings that I have within me where I want to be held and loved by another man do not mean that I am a homosexual." I tell them "no", that they are not homosexual. God did not make us that way. That word homosexual means that we can only be healthy if we have a physical sexual relationship with a same-sex partner. That is not the way God made us. One young man asked, "What is this drive within me or this need within me?" I said, "The need within you is for you to be held by a father who simply wants to bless you and pattern for you the life of a father. That is what it is. The need within you is a need to please another man, and the goal in that is for you to please Father God. The distortion is when the relationship degenerates to where you find yourself attempting to physically please another man. But that is not God's plan."

The young men seemed pleased and quite relieved at my explanation. The world says that there is such a thing as a homosexual but the Bible says there is sin called sodomy. The sin of sodomy is where two people have a same-sex physical sexual relationship. Romans 1 says that God will give men and women over to degrading passions if they do not turn themselves over to God and begin to grow in grace and in the knowledge of the Lord Jesus Christ. That is why our society today is in trouble, because we have not seen the necessity of growing spiritually.

Now, the good news is that if there is someone who has fallen into that trap, they can get out. How does a person who has found himself or herself in a homosexual relationship get out of it? By coming back to Father God and saying, "Father God, I want to please You," and then be born again and be established as a child of God who then transitions upward in maturity. There are those today who are being set free because they understand that Father God will give them His life and they can therefore please God.

Sometimes in ministry we can get our attitudes towards people twisted too. I received a letter from a pastor who said that he wanted to thank me because some years ago I showed him that he was to stop trying to please people and begin pleasing God. He said he had been trying to serve God and please people. When he understood and corrected his direction he said it set him free in his ministry to come to the place where he didn't have to please people any more. It is good for us when we come to the place where we understand that we don't have to please people anymore. Why? We won't fear the faces of men and can then minister the truth in love.

Some years ago a woman who was arthritic and had a host of other physical problems, came to our home for prayer. My wife and I placed her in a chair in our living room and prayed for her. The Spirit of the Lord came on me with a word of knowledge and showed me that this woman was in a lesbian relationship. So I said, "You know, I believe that the Lord has said something to me and wants to set you free. I believe that your problem is caused by what the Holy Spirit just showed me." I asked her if I could tell her about it. She said, "Yes." So I went on, saying, "The Holy Spirit has shown me that you are in a lesbian relationship with another woman." She immediately jumped to her feet, defensive. She cried, "You can't tell me there is anything wrong with that, scripturally!" to which, I replied, "I can point to you plenty of scriptures showing that it is a sin." With angry eyes fixed firmly upon me, she said, "I want to tell you this right now. This other woman understands me. She loves me."

Now that was a very vivid description to me of a childish attitude. A childish attitude is one in which you look for people who understand you and accept you and make you feel comfortable. A sonship attitude is one where you serve others and change lives. You minister from Father God's point of view. If we are always relating in life on the basis of who and what will make us comfortable and feel good, then we will get trapped. We never come out of that and we never move into the place where God wants us to be.

I said to the woman, "If you were relating to a man as your husband instead of relating to this woman, then you would be relating to someone that you have to minister to. You have to change and be different. But you are not changing. You are relating to this woman on the basis of what she can do for you and you continue just as you are and never change. The problem with this is that the Spirit of God in you is telling you that it is wrong and that you need to repent. You need to step out of it and when you do, I believe that God will heal you." Instead of doing that, she stormed out of the house and never came back. Afterwards, any time she saw me, she turned and went the other way. She would not listen. But it has been good to see some people listen at times and see the changes that take place in their lives as they come into wholeness through the word of God.

If you are a person who never had a father or mother to hold and love you when you were a child or you had parents that, when they held you they abused you, you need to know that you can be healed and be made whole in Jesus Christ. You may say, "Well, how can I be healed, pastor?" By crawling into the arms of Jesus and beginning to worship and bless Him. As you praise the name of God and worship through the blood of Jesus Christ, the Holy Spirit begins to rise up in you. He will cause you to begin to cry, "Abba Father!" Healing will begin to take place in your spirit. Then as a son of God (this includes both genders), you can look back on those parents whose lives had been distorted and say, "I forgive my mother and father and I bless them in the name of Jesus. I pray God's blessings on their lives and release them from what they did to me." Then you can move into wholeness as a son of God and begin relating on the basis of that sonship.

The second goal of sonship is developing faith for living. What is the foundation of faith? On what basis is faith built? Now Jesus called great faith the ability to work under authority. That is what sonship is all about. Sonship is coming to a place in your life where you make a decision that you are going to obey Father God. A good place to begin to obey Father God is putting yourself in a place where you are accountable to some other people and you do what you are supposed to do. For instance, if you are an employee, as long as your employer does not call on you to compromise your faith and conviction, then you can do a good job, making sure you are on time, giving him 100%. In the church, you can honor and respect those who are in spiritual authority in the church. By so doing, honor and maturity begins to develop in your spirit and the Holy Spirit sees this and it brings the favor of God into your life.

I once knew a young man who did just that. He came into a church and said that he wanted to minister and asked how he could best minister. They gave him some menial tasks to do and saw that he was faithful completing them. He did what he was supposed to do. As his faithfulness was revealed, slowly but surely the leaders of that church began raising him up and soon he became a leader in the church. Why? Because he understood how authority operates. He was able to come under authority and learn how to submit himself to authority so that he could see what authority meant in his life.

In Luke 10:17, Jesus took seventy of His men and sent them out two-by-two to minister. These men came back and said, "Even the demons are subject to us in your name." Jesus said to them that He watched Satan fall from heaven like lightening. In other words, He saw that they had authority over Satan. "Behold I have given you authority to tread upon serpents and scorpions and over all the power of the enemy and nothing shall injure you. Nevertheless do not rejoice in this that the spirits are subject to you, but rejoice that your names are recorded in heaven." Then in verse 21, at that time Jesus rejoiced greatly in the Holy Spirit and said, "I praise you Father, Lord of heaven and earth, that you did hide these things from the wise and intelligent and have revealed them to babes." He is saying that these seventy men were sent out as babes so that they could become sons. They discovered something when they went out. They went out in the name of the Lord. They submitted to the authority of the Lord Jesus Christ and in the name of Jesus, they discovered that they could cast out demons and heal the sick. They came back rejoicing in that and Jesus put them into proper balance by saying, "Don't rejoice in that but rejoice in the fact that your name is written in heaven." Jesus went on to say, "Father, I thank you that you have revealed this to these babes." Why? Because the babes were destined to become sons, then husbands, and then fathers in the faith.

Jesus had a plan for those seventy men but that plan was going to be achieved on the basis of their willingness to submit to the authority of the Lord Jesus Christ. It is that authority that is so necessary in our lives. Without it we are not going to change or grow. If you don't have spiritual authority working in your life that you can submit to and work under, you are not going to grow spiritually. You might as well take that and log it away because it is a fact. It is true that if you do not have spiritual authority, if you are a maverick and independent and you are running around on your own and you don't have authorities in your life to whom you can submit in a healthy way within the body of Christ, then you are not going to grow the way you are supposed to grow in your life. If you don't have a submission to the Lordship of Jesus Christ and to the Holy Spirit, then you are not going to grow the way you are supposed to grow in your life.

We all have room to grow. There are so many things that we could be doing in the body of Christ if authority was established among the people. We have difficulty getting people to be committed to their work, to be faithful to what they say they will do. You get some people committed to do something for a period of time, but it is hard to get them to be faithful in showing up to do the things that they have committed themselves to do. It could be getting them committed to work in the nursery. It could be a commitment to other ministries in the church and they feel no obligation at all to be faithful to the commitment. Then they come and say, "God, what is wrong in my life?"

The truth of the matter is that what is wrong is that they are not submitting to authority. By submitting to it, I mean, if you come to me and say we need help in a certain area, in a certain part of the ministry, and I say I will do it, my submission is that I will do it. If I don't do it then I am not submitted to the Lord. If I have no responsibility at all in the body of Christ then where is the authority in my life? If all I have to do is come and sit and listen to the Word and leave and I have nothing for which I am accountable, then where is the authority in my life? My accountability is that I put myself in a place where I am responsible to do something in the name of Jesus. And it means that I am accountable for that pledge and therefore responsible to give an answer to someone. If the person I am responsible to says that we need to have a meeting, then I don't get upset by it. I do everything I can to attend the meeting.

The first goal of sonship is developing the pattern of fatherhood where we begin to take on His characteristics. The second is developing faith where you discover that you can cast out demons and pray for the sick and Jesus will heal them. The third is faithfulness; being faithful in what we do.

There is a good example given by Jesus of what faithfulness entails. Matthew 21:23 says, "When He had come into the temple, the chief priests and the elders of the people came to Him as He was teaching and said, 'by what authority are you doing these things and who gave you this authority?'" They did not question whether He had authority. They didn't say, "Do you have authority to do this?" They said, "By what authority are you doing this and who gave you this authority?" They recognized that Jesus was under authority. They recognized that He was submitted to someone. That is the strength of His ministry, that He was always submitted to the Father. He always obeyed the Holy Spirit. So Jesus answered and said to them in verse 24, "I will ask you one thing, which if you tell me I will also tell you by what authority I do these things."

This is what Jesus asked them: "The baptism of John was from what source, from heaven or man?" You may think, what does that question have to do with Jesus having authority? Well, today we have to explain baptism to a lot of people. There are people who know nothing about baptism. But in Jesus' day, He did not have to explain baptism to the Pharisees. They all understood clearly the baptism of John. The Jewish people practiced a baptism of repentance. It was a cleansing rite and they actually baptized by immersion, so when John the Baptist walked out in the middle of the Jordan River, raised his voice and began to preach and say, "Repent and prepare for the coming of the Messiah," the people knew what to do---- repent! They were to turn their focus away from sin and turn it to the Messiah. They walked into the water and submitted themselves to John the Baptist and he baptized them. As he baptized them and put them under the water, they were acknowledging their willingness to be submitted to God. Now, the Pharisees knew that John's baptism was from heaven; they knew that it was a godly act but they began reasoning among themselves, saying, "If we say from heaven He will say to us, 'Why then did you not believe him?' But if we say from man, we fear the multitude, for they say that John is a prophet and he was speaking for God." In answering Jesus, they said that they did not know. By saying this, they were saying, "We do not assume any responsibility for this and we will not submit to your authority. We ignore what you say." That is what these men did. Jesus said, "Then neither will I tell you by what authority I do these things."

Why wouldn't Jesus tell them by what authority he did it? Because He knew that they wouldn't receive it, anyway. They were not about to receive it. All they wanted to do was trick Jesus and trip Him up. Then He proceeds on. He says in verse 28, "But what do you think? A man had two sons and he came to the first and said, 'Son, go work today in the vineyard,' and he answered, and said, 'I will sir,' but he did not go." In other words, the farmer said to his son, "We have a lot of work to do in the field, go work in the field." So the son said, "All right Dad, I will go." And then he watched out of the corner of his eye, and when his dad went around the barn and headed back to the house, he said, "Now I will do what I want to do." And he didn't go work in the field. Then the farmer came to the second son (verse 30) and said the same thing: "Son, we have a lot of work to do in the field, go work in the vineyard." The son answered, saying, "I will not", yet afterward regretted it and went. He was saying, "Even though I don't like doing it, I am going to do it." This is a classic contrast of the difference between one son who was a child and the other who was a son. The child did what he wanted to do. He ignored what father said. The son obeyed and honored his father.

Have you ever said to a child, don't touch that and he touched it anyway? That is not sonship. Coming to the place where I say, "If I disobey God, that will cost me something." That is not sonship, that is childhood. Sonship is when you come to the place where you say, "Father God wants me to do this and whether I like it or not, I am going to do it because I want to submit to Him. He is Lord over my life. I want to please Him."

So Jesus said to them, "Which of the two did the will of the Father?" They replied, "The one who said, 'I don't like working in the field,' but he did it. Jesus said to them, "Truly I say to you that the tax gatherers and the harlots will get into the kingdom of God before you. For John came to you in the way of righteousness and you did not believe him but the tax gatherers and harlots did believe him." You see, they did not even feel remorse, even after rejecting John's message. Jesus was saying that when a tax gatherer, a sinner and a harlot came to the place where they realized that they needed the Father, they repented and did it God's way.

What about a self-righteous person? What will he do? A self-righteous person does it his way and not God's way. Children are self-righteous. Sons are repentant. You may say, "Well, how can a child be self-righteous?" Have you ever walked into a room where something has just happened and two children are standing in opposite corners looking guilty? You say, "Which one of you did it?" They each point an accusing finger at the other.

A child is self-righteous but a son is always repentant and submitted to the Father and that makes the difference. In sonship, God wants to bring us to the place where He can turn our inheritance over to us. In childhood, God cannot turn our inheritance over to us. All He can do is give to us when we ask. In our childhood, in the kingdom of God, we have to ask God and then He gives it to us if it is good for us. In sonship, we come to the place where we no longer ask, we begin to give, discovering that it is more blessed to give than to receive.

Luke 15:11-15 tells the story of the prodigal son. The prodigal son asked for his inheritance and then showed that he was not a son at all, but a child. What did he do with the inheritance? He wasted every bit of it. He spent it all on loose living. Later, he came back and said to his father, "I am not worthy to be called a son, make me a hired servant. Bring me back and let me start all over." That is the essence of new birth.

But what about the older brother? In verse 28, the son has come back and the father had the fatted calf killed and the older brother saw all of this going on. The older brother then became angry and was not willing to go in the house. His father came out and entreated the older brother to come in the house. This brother answered and said to his father, "For many years I have been serving you and I have never neglected a command of yours, and yet you have never given me a kid that I can make merry with my friends but when this son of yours came who devoured your wealth with harlots, you killed the fatted calf for him." In verse 31, look at what his father said: "My child". He did not say, "My son". Why? Because this older brother now was acting like a child. What was he doing? He was judging his father's love on the basis of what father was doing for this repentant brother. And a child always judges the parent's love on the basis of what the parents do for the other children. But not a son. The parents do something for the other child and this child says, "Where is mine." Then he gets jealous and complains, saying, "You did it for him, what about me?" The son is glad that his brother is blessed.

That happens sometimes within the body of Christ. When the Spirit of God begins to move through someone with anointing others become jealous. "Well, what about me? Why doesn't God work through me?" Sometimes there can be jealousy between ministers.

When I was in college, I was invited to pastor a church four miles away. It was a nice church with over 300 members. It was about this time that an acquaintance, a fellow student, quit speaking to me for a year. Finally he began to speak and so I took the opportunity to ask, "Why haven't you been speaking to me?" He said that he thought he was supposed to have the church. For one whole year he had been jealous. He was not able to speak to me until he was called to a church of his own. He had lost the joy in the Lord because he had judged himself on the basis of what God had done for me. We both wanted to pastor churches.

There is jealousy sometimes among the leadership in the church. That is what this son was going through. Let's see what the father said to the older son. In verse 31, the father said to him, "My son, you have always been with me and all that is mine is yours." All that is God's is not the child's. Galatians 4 says that God puts a child under management. And a manager controls his life and gets what God wants him to have, but not a child. All that the father has now belongs to the son. Do you know what the father does? When you decide to become a son, Father says, "Son, here are the keys to the warehouse. Use whatever you need in order to do my work." Why? Because the Father knows that he is now a son and is not committed to indulge himself, so the Father trusts him. If the Father gave him the keys to the warehouse and the son went in and began to devour the contents or threw it away as did the prodigal son, the Father could not give him the keys. He gives him the keys because he has become a son and the son now begins to take on the characteristics of the Father. He begins to think like the Father. The Father is thinking, "What can I do for the servants?" What does this one need, what does that one need? So He gives the keys to the son who is His junior partner and says, "Son everything in there is ours together. You work the way I work. You think the way I think. You help me out." So the son begins to take that which belongs to Father and becomes a steward and a partner and develops it. His whole orientation in life now is built on the concept of giving and not receiving. He no longer judges himself on the basis of what Father does for his brother but on the basis of what Father's will is for everyone. He says to the older son, "You have been with Me always and all that is Mine is yours. We have to be merry and rejoice because your brother was dead and has been born again. He was dead and has begun to live. He was lost and has been found."

That is the essence of sonship. God loves us so much that He is going to bring us into sonship one way or another. In Hebrews 12:4, the writer is talking about resisting temptations of life, and says, "You have not yet resisted to the point of shedding blood in your striving against sin; and you have forgotten the exhortation which is addressed to you as sons. My son, do not regard lightly the discipline of the Lord nor faint when you are reproved by Him. It is important for you to have the discipline to be under the authority of the Lord. For those whom the Lord loves, He disciplines and scourges. Every son whom He receives, it is for discipline that you endure; God deals with you as sons; for what son is there whom his father does not discipline. If you are without discipline of which all have become partakers, then you are illegitimate children and not sons. Furthermore, we have earthly fathers that disciplined us and we respected them; shall we not much rather be subject to the Father of spirits and live? For they disciplined us for a short time as seemed best to them, but He disciplines us for our good, so that we may share His holiness. All discipline for the moment seems not to be joyful, but sorrowful; yet to those who have been trained by it, afterwards it yields the peaceful fruit of righteousness."

God has a plan to bring us to the place where He can turn our inheritance over to us because He trusts us with it and because we act like sons. How do we come to that place where we can achieve this? We do it through submission to the lordship of Jesus Christ. We do it by making a decision to become responsible;

to acknowledge authority over our lives. Jesus is not only savior but He is Lord of our lives.

The mother said she nearly fainted one day because her son asked for the keys to the garage and came out pushing the lawnmower. That is sonship. How about us? When we say, "God, give me your keys, pour out your blessings on me." Do we come out driving the sports car or pushing the lawnmower? I pray that we come out pushing the lawnmower, thereby taking on our responsibilities before Father God and doing what He wants us to do.

I believe that real problems can be broken in our lives by making the decision to submit to the authority of Father God and by putting ourselves in the place where we are responsible and accountable to someone in the body of Christ. If we will do this, our phones will be ringing in the church office with people saying, "You give me something to do." If you want God to move in your life, just do that. Say, "I will not allow myself to eat at the Lord's table and never become a son and never learn to give. I refuse to do that!" You can say that you have a right according to this scripture to say to the leaders and the pastors, "I require you in the name of Jesus to put me to work. You will not deprive me of my sonship. So you find a place for me and put me to work." A talent survey can be done to see exactly where you fit in. Pray and ask the Holy Spirit to show your pastor just where you fit in and when he says, "Here", you can say, "Thank you, I will take it. Give me the keys to it and show me how to get it done." Then you can say, "Lord, I expect good things to happen out of this!" and you can say to the devil, "I don't have time for you to pester me with all of the problems of anger, resentment and self-pity. I am moving on with God. I am moving out as a son of God. I am no longer a child. I am not controlled by the devil but controlled by the Spirit of God."

3

HUSBANDSHIP

Husbandship, the third stage in christian growth is described in 2 John 2:10 which says, "That the one who loves his brother abides in the light and there is no cause for stumbling in him." That is God's description of husbandship: The ability to manage a one-on-one relationship so that you can represent Father God in His affairs as one of his partners. In verse 11, John says "The one who hates his brother is in the darkness and walks in the darkness and does not know where he is going because the darkness has blinded his eyes." And then in verses 12 and 13, he describes the other three stages: "I am writing to you, little children, because your sins are forgiven you for His name's sake. I am writing to you, fathers, because you know Him who has been from the beginning. I am writing to you, young men, because you have overcome the evil one." In verses 12 and 13, three stages are described: 1) childhood, 2) sonship, and 3) fatherhood. And then back in verse 10, we see God's description of husbandship.

We need to understand that a husband is a manager. First Timothy 3:1 says, "It is a trustworthy statement: if any man aspires to the office of father in the church"-----that is, overseer-----"it is a fine work that he desires to do." In further describing the husband, verse 4 says in part, "He must be one who manages his own household well...." He is saying that the father must be one who has successfully transitioned from childhood into sonship, has been proven in husbandship, and has therefore moved into fatherhood. His husbandship proves that he has the gift of God for management of life's relationships.

Our goal should be to achieve fatherhood within the body of Christ. In order to do that, we commit ourselves to successfully transition from childhood to sonship and then finally, husbandship. A child, you will remember, is a slave to his circumstances. A child reacts to provocation instead of acting by the Word of God. A child compares himself to other people instead of being sent forth by God. A son is a junior partner with God. He breaks away from his self-centeredness and begins to see from Father's point of view. A son willfully submits himself to the authority of Father and in that submission, learns what partnership is all about. We have already seen in sonship that when we begin to discover the power of God, when we discover we can cast out demons in the name of Jesus, we can lay hands on the sick and they are healed, when we discover that we can proclaim the gospel of Jesus Christ, then we have become in effect, a son. And as a son, we also have the fruit of the spirit. We learn how, in love, to bless and encourage other people.

Now, the evidence that we have been freed from our childhood, from our self-centeredness, to where we have become God-centered, relating to people as God relates to them, is always revealed in our husbandship, not in our sonship. And that is a mistake that the church has made. Oftentimes the churches have set into fatherhood persons in whom the gifts of the Spirit have begun to operate, thereby making the mistake in thinking that, because the gifts of the Spirit are present in their lives, they are mature leaders. But we have seen that the operation of the gifts simply means that they are moving into sonship operating in partnership with God.

A husband is a manager of relationships, developing the ability to achieve the highest good for other people, including the exercising of authority. I am discovering that the further I go in working with leaders in other churches that people do not understand that authority also works in mutual submission one to another. For instance, in order for authority to operate in my home, not only must my wife submit to me but I must submit to her, as well. Our children must engage in that submission also. There are certain areas where I honor, respect, and acknowledge my wife's ability to have a part in the home and in that relationship.

What about in the church? What about the

eldership of the church? Wherein does the authority rest in the church? Is it that the elders come in and sit down before the pastor and he tells them what to do and they do it? Is that the expression of authority? Not at all. Authority rests in the fact that the pastor and the elders come together and pray. And being committed to the body of Christ, they mutually seek to know the mind of Christ. That is the essence of authority. Authority does not rest in the democratic vote. The democratic vote is an expression of the will of the people. If we come together as elders and say that the majority rules, we get the will of the people. But when we come together committed to seeking the mind of Christ and working together until a consensus is reached by the entire body, then we know the Lord has spoken.

In Acts 13:2 we read about a gathering of Christian leaders at the Church at Antioch during which the Holy Spirit said, "Send forth Paul and Barnabas to the work to which I have appointed them." When agreement settles over the body and there is a consensus among everyone that this indeed is the mind of Christ, we begin working under authority and are able to submit to each other as together we say, "The Lord is speaking." I have discovered in a meeting that one brother will have the Word of the Lord and generally this is what he will say: "I don't feel peace in my spirit about this which we are considering but I want the rest of you to know that if that is what you want to do, then I will go along with it." My elders will attest to the fact that time-and-time again, I have said to them that we will wait and pray until we find out whether this is of the Lord. In that way, we submit to the authority of Christ and honor each other.

What does a child do? A child does not submit to anyone. Take a child who skips over sonship, thereby failing to understand how to work with Father God, and then you put him in relationship with other people. As soon as the people in whom he is trying to relate disagree with what he wants to do, he does what a child does. Sometimes when children are babies and do not get their way, they fall on the floor and begin screaming; screaming while their little bodies spin round-and-round until they topple to the floor.

Oftentimes, we as adults act in the same manner. Usually when we are in disagreement with someone it is an indicator that we have not been successfully developed in our sonship. We have made the leap directly from childhood into husbandship thereby never having been stripped of our self-centeredness. Father God has given to us the Holy Spirit in order to bring us to the place where we can function in husbandship. Husbandship is that laboratory in which the Lord puts us to test us in order for Him to determine whether or not we are ready for fatherhood.

Many of the problems in our nation today rest in the fact that men have never been set free from their childhood but have, instead, bypassed sonship and have gone directly to husbandship, yet they are still consumed with self-centeredness. As soon as a situation arises which requires them to submit in a mutual relationship to their wives, they abdicate and walk away. Some play golf, some drink, while others pursue a variety of avenues of avoidance. They abdicate.

I once talked to one man who said that he was so busy that he could never get home. When we got down to the root of it, he admitted that he always had time to do other things that he wanted to do. But the reason that he could not go home was because at home, there was someone who required him to be accountable in a one-on-one relationship. Who are you? What are you doing? Where are you going? When will you be back? This accountability is important in our lives. It is one of the major responsibilities of the husband. Accountability provides stability.

We find that the Bible makes it clear that God is a manager, a husband. In Jeremiah 31:31, the Lord says, "'Behold the days are coming,' declares the Lord, 'when I will make a new covenant with the house of Israel and with the house of Judah, not like the covenant that I made with their fathers in the day I took them by the hand to bring them out of the land of Egypt. My covenant which they broke, although I was a husband to them.'" So God says that He is a husband. We can say then that God operates in husbandship and it is His husbandship that demonstrates to us that God is a father. And in that husbandship we discover God's loving care and His management over us.

Now, we can learn something about management in life if we ask, "How does God manage?" God is a manager. What does God do in his management, anyway? I want to give you the key to God's managerial methods. God always manages on the basis of covenant. Always! The foundation of God's management methods is that of covenant. God can manage all of your sins and he can take care of them on the basis of covenant. You come into covenant with Him through the blood of Jesus and God will take care of your sins. When you come into covenant with Him on the basis of the blood of Jesus Christ, God takes care of your bad habits. You yield to Him every day. God relates on the basis of covenant. That covenant involves a mutual submission. The expression of covenant is found in Genesis 14, 15, 16 and 17 when God cut covenant with Abraham. In that covenant God laid His life down for Abraham by way of animal sacrifice. Just as God made covenant with Abraham through blood sacrifice, God has made covenant with us through the blood of Christ.

So God's management skill is based on blood covenant and includes first of all the submission of God to us. You say that is almost sacrilegious. Well, look and see who is hanging on the cross and who cries out, "My God, my God, why hast thou forsaken me." God loves us so much that He came and laid down His life in Christ Jesus on the cross.

Our problem in attempting to become husbands and managers in life is that we are always defensive and self-protective, but God's management says in His covenant relationships that He is open and vulnerable and always ready to be injured and hurt. Then the covenant is established by God and it is shared with us by Jesus Christ. He comes to us and says, "You come to me." He establishes what the New Testament calls a body of believers. That body of believers is established through covenant and we come into a mutual submission to each other where we honor the presence of the Holy Spirit within each other's life and we are made whole. In that covenant relationship we enter into what we call confrontation.

I would like to explain the difference between confrontation and conflict. Back in the mid 70's I wrote a book for Logos International. They published and released it in the United States, Canada and England. They asked me to write a book for them dealing with a crisis in the charismatic renewal on discipleship and how to maintain good discipleship in churches. I wrote the book during the time when the church was in crisis around the nation as well as other countries over relationships and submission. As a result, the leaders of the movement felt that we were out of balance. Understanding their error and the problems it created challenged me. I met with those leaders for two hours in Dallas, Texas. They were saying that I was the one who was in error, and that I had misrepresented who they were and what they were doing. I said, "Okay, if that is the case, if you would write a letter to me, telling me how I misrepresented who and what you are, I will correct my error in the next printing of the book." (The book had been sold out and was to be reprinted.)

Instead of writing a letter to me as I had requested, these men gathered their intellectuals, critiqued my book and wrote a letter to the publisher in Painesville, New Jersey, demanding that the book be removed from the market. The publisher refused the request and kept it on the market. Shortly thereafter, I walked into a meeting in a large conference. The people were breaking up into groups of eighteen men each, and I was assigned to one of the groups. When I walked into the room where my assigned group was meeting, I discovered that I was the last one to arrive. There was one vacant chair remaining and-----you guessed it-----it was right next to the same leader of the organization that had tried to have my book taken off the market.

So when I sat down, the tension in the air was inescapable. There happened to be a man just across the room who, although a stranger to me, knew the leader of the disciple organization because the leader was nationally-acclaimed. The man said, "You two men are going to have to do something about this confrontation." Well, I had already been teaching that confrontation is healthy, that you must have confrontation in order to grow and if you do not learn how to deal with conflict, you will never grow emotionally and spiritually in life. You must allow confrontation into your life and let it work for your good.

So, it aroused the attention of the other men at the table when this man, who wore a clerical collar, looked at us and said, "You two men must deal with this confrontation." Sitting next to him was a psychiatrist from Detroit, Michigan. When he spoke, peace came into my spirit. He said, "Brother, you must be talking about conflict. If there is something going on between these two men, they must have confrontation. They must face each other and deal with it. They must lay it out on the table and say, 'You are wrong here,' until they finally come to the place where they can receive what God is saying to them." He went on to say that conflict is where each person entrenches himself and refuses to give. They are inflexible and just butt heads. That is conflict. He said, "Now, what I think these two men need to do is get alone and talk." This was a confrontational-type meeting of national leaders. We followed the assignment and got together and talked.

Later, I flew to Dallas, Texas, years after our confrontation and walked into a meeting of a network of Christian ministries and sat down at the board table and this same man with whom I had the confrontation walked in and sat down beside me. I knew when he sat down that the crisis was over and the confrontation had brought healing.

If you run from confrontation, you will never be healed. However you must avoid conflict which is destructive and will not heal you. Confrontation in our lives is good and necessary. In Romans 12:18, the Bible says, "If possible, so far as it depends on you, be at peace with all men." You cannot be at peace with all men. There are some people who have conflict natures. You cannot be at peace with a conflict-oriented person. There are some people who were born and raised in conflict. They have never learned the difference between conflict and confrontation. But you can, if you are able to help that person come to the point of confrontation, you can help them heal.

Recently when I was in a meeting with some elders and their pastor it was evident that there was conflict between them. I laid the groundwork based upon faith in being able to all know the mind of Christ. Present were a business man, an attorney, a retired engineer, the pastor and I. By talking, we laid the groundwork. Once the groundwork for confrontation was established, the Holy Spirit moved on that meeting, bringing healing in their relationships. Before, when they were conflict-oriented, they drifted deeper and deeper into the problem, moving further and further apart. But confrontation brought healing.

Problems come from the failure to successfully

transition from childhood into sonship, resulting in conflict oriented lives instead of confrontation oriented lives. Here are examples of some of the problems: The self-centeredness in the child who has not been freed from self-centeredness produces conflict in future relationships, thereby causing the child to go from one conflict to another. We may enter a romantic relationship, thinking it is going to be wonderful but then demands are placed upon us. We refuse to submit to a mutual relationship and be healed confrontationally. The conflict breaks the relationship. So we move on and find a new person, a new relationship. This cycle also happens in churches and other places. When you are confrontational instead of conflicting, you can go anywhere. Because you have the ability to dialogue, you have the ability to speak the truth in love one to another and thereby you have the ability to make a relationship work. When you live as God's order of faith and practice directs, you can live peacefully so that, as far as it depends on you, you are at peace with others. So the first example is that a child, the person who enters into husbandship without going through sonship, will enter in with a conflict-oriented nature, repeatedly resisting efforts to be healed in one-on-one relationships, thereby being unable to manage those relationships.

Secondly, in many cases, the child who has moved out of his secure surroundings, will revert back to nurturing his natural instincts. The natural instinct could be anger, unhealthy sexual relationships, or possibly relationships which are homosexual in nature. I have already said that, biblically, there is no such thing as a homosexual. There is a sin of sodomy where people of the same sex engage in sexual acts and God says that it is sin, just as adultery is sin. They engage in activities where they attempt to be personally confirmed and physical stimulation of some type develops. It may be through pornography. It could be through romance novels where they vicariously enter into the romantic relationships of other people. It could be the addiction to movies. But whatever it is, they gravitate to the area that nurtures their natural instincts, just like a child. A child gets nervous and sticks his thumb into his mouth. We adults don't stick out thumbs in our mouths, we just do something else which possibly gets us into trouble. Immature and undeveloped personality characteristics in husbandship will be expressed in physical ways.

What are the benefits of successfully transitioning from childhood, through sonship into husbandship? First of all, you discover who you really are. You never know who you are until you come into husbandship. I did not know who I was until I married. Then I discovered not so much who the girl was that I had married but who the man was that she had married. Sometimes I did not like it because, in attempting to relate to her, I revealed who I really was. Now, I have had people come and say, "Life was just great until I joined the church and then everything began to fall apart." No it didn't. When you joined the church, you were born again and the Lord gave you a period of time to enjoy being a child. Then one day the Holy Spirit began to pull you into sonship, trying to move you into management of relationships. You began to discover who you really were and didn't like it. You had suppressed that person within you and concealed the true nature but now the Holy Spirit was requiring you to come forth into maturity. You could either continue to be conflict-oriented or you could say, "Praise God for the confrontation." If you don't have someone who can confront you, then find some people and say, "Speak truth to me in Jesus' name. I am ready to be changed and to grow into fatherhood in the Lord's house." So we discover who we really are. We know our true identity in relationships. First we discover who we really are. We come into wholeness and authority is released to accomplish the will of God.

When husbandship begins to reveal your faults and weaknesses, what should you do? You may come into husbandship and discover that you are an angry person. You may discover that you are resentful or critical or lustful. What do you do? The first step is to go back and strengthen the foundations that are revealed to be weak. Just like the prodigal, who went back to father's house and said to his father that he did not deserve to be a son and to make him a hired servant. He asked his father to let him return to stage one. Second, we repent of the rebellion in our nature. 1 Samuel 15:23 says, "For rebellion is as the sin of witchcraft." So, all witchcraft is rooted in rebellion, beginning with rebellion against God. So we deal with it. Then we repent and submit ourselves to God and to the body of Christ. That repentance becomes a growth facilitator, encouraging our transition into healthy husbandship and fatherhood. Once we do that, we make a commitment to grow and thereafter, we can call every activity that we have in the church which involves one-on-one relationships, growth groups. That is what they should be. So we commit ourselves to growth. We accept the fact that confrontation is given as a gift of God, as a healthy instrument, to reveal our true nature. We commit ourselves to honor authority and to honor God. Malachi 3 talks about honoring God. We are not honoring God if we are not good stewards to God with all of our resources. Then we intentionally adopt the patterns of mature fatherhood and begin to act like father acts. Here is a guarantee: if you will adopt godly attitudes and, for three months, intentionally live by them, you will be a different person. However you cannot follow them for just one day. Bad habits are not broken in one day. It takes time.

4

FATHERHOOD

In 1 John 2:13, John writes, "I am writing to you, fathers, because you know Him who has been from the beginning..." (Fatherhood). We have discussed the first three steps to maturity. We will now take a look at the final step-----fatherhood.

Who is a father, anyway? A father is one who is responsible for the formation of character in another person. A child is a slave to his circumstances. We have seen that a child reacts emotionally to provocation. He cannot handle relationships. He understands life only in reference to himself and understands much of life only in reference to his own natural well-being so that when he is disturbed, he expresses himself in natural ways. Often with your own children, you may note that they have a need and are restless because of some manifestation in the natural or perhaps you notice an altering of their habits. Or it could be some personality quirk that manifests itself that lets you know that they are under stress, that they need help. We tend to gravitate toward natural stimulation in order to assure and encourage ourselves. We have seen that a son is a junior partner with his father. He begins to act according to the father's will. He takes on the father's characteristics. Instead of being self-centered, he becomes God-centered and becomes concerned about the affairs of father. He is interested in carrying out the work of his father and seeing that it is advanced so that he is now free from self-preservation and becomes enamored with the things of father. We have seen that a husband is a manager of life. He demonstrates that he can manage one-on-one relationships. He manages as a representative of father. A manager is a husband. He is a steward and it is here that we enter into the laboratory where we test our ability to function as mature believers in Christ.

First John says that, if you say that you love God but you cannot get along with your brother, the love of God is not in you, that you have not gone beyond your childhood. So we prove to ourselves whether or not we have successfully transitioned from childhood into sonship by the way we manage one-on-one relationships. This transition is important in preparing us for the fourth step of maturity-----fatherhood.

Now, a father is an overseer. A father sets the patterns for living. A father is God-centered and is one who is concerned about others but not about himself. Let's clear up a misconception about the fatherhood of God. I have heard it said at times that God is like a father, but nothing could be further from the truth. God is not like a father. God is not like anyone. God is God and is the only model of true fatherhood. The goal is that we become like father God, taking on His characteristics and coming to know Him in Jesus Christ.

Now, fatherhood defines patterns for living. A father is a person who is responsible for the formation of character in another person. So that is our goal when we go through these different stages in order to come to the place where we can assume responsibility and can mature to the place where we can say to those for whom we are responsible: "Until you learn to walk in fatherhood, do what I do. Model yourself after me."

Jesus said in Matthew 5:48 to be mature as your father in heaven is mature. The King James version says to be perfect as your father in heaven is perfect, but the word there for perfect is "teleioi" which means "to come into a maturity", a state of growth in which you have passed through these stages and come to the place where you are modeling the life of the Father. So God is the true Father and all other forms of fatherhood are to pattern themselves after Him.

In Ephesians 3: 14, 15, Paul is praying and giving us understanding of fatherhood in the Kingdom of God. He says, "For this reason I bow my knees before the Father," the "patera" in the Greek. That is where we get the name "Papa". It is right out of this concept of fatherhood. "I bow my knees before the

Father from whom every family in heaven and on earth derives its name." It is interesting that the word "family" is the word "patria" in the Greek. It is a derivative of the word "father". So actually, Paul is saying, "For this reason I bow my knees before the Father from whom every fatherhood in heaven and on earth derives its name, that He would grant you according to the riches of His glory in this fatherhood within the family of God, to be strengthened with power through His Spirit in the inner man so that Christ may dwell in your hearts through faith and that you, being rooted and grounded in love, may be able to comprehend with all the saints, what is the breadth, length, height and depth and to know the love of Christ which surpasses knowledge, that you may be filled up with all the fullness of God."

Now, to know God is to come into a relationship where the life of the "pater" is flowing through you and then the body of Christ begins to experience and enjoy the fatherhood. The Fatherhood of God is known and understood as His life flows through the body and people are raised up into the state of being fathers within the church. Paul says in Romans 8:19, "All of nature groans, waiting for the manifestation or the unveiling or the revealing of the sons of God." Why? Because it is then known that when we become sons, we have been freed, delivered, stripped of our self-centeredness and are now on the way to becoming fathers in the faith. God's goal is for you to be a father in the faith. Whether you are a man or woman, you are to come to a place where you experience a part of the "patrea" of God. "I bow my knees before the father from whom every fatherhood in heaven and on earth derives its name." So God's goal is for us to come to that state while the Holy Spirit continues working on us until we finally release everything to the Father and let Him free us of our self-centeredness and selfishness. When we do, we begin moving up beside the Father and getting a perspective of life from His point of view. We begin to see what He sees. We begin to understand more of what He understands and find our entire approach to life changing. We are no longer looking at life from the perspective of what it can do to meet our needs but from what we can do to meet the needs of others. We have moved into fatherhood.

Fatherhood is important in the church as well. For without a fatherhood being established, the church remains weak and confused with divisions and separations occurring because the church is void of a source of mature guidance. Then problems arise within bodies of believers because people have been raised up into positions of fatherhood who are not fathers in the faith. So when they face difficulties, problems and serious decisions, they display selfish opinions because they are childish in their nature and are not fathers. They do not know the Father. And if they do not know the Father then they do not know the Father's will. And so they find themselves expressing their own will and opinions. When the fathers start separating and dividing, they divide the body, they divide the family. Some will follow one leader, others will follow another while still others follow yet a third leader. When these problems then are manifested outside help is needed. We form a presbytery to help church leaders in conflict. The leaders are not functioning in their fatherhood. If they were, they would not need fathers from the outside to come and define a fatherhood for them.

That is what a presbytery is-----a fatherhood. We establish a fatherhood because those leaders are not functioning in that fatherhood role. Therefore the body, not having that fatherhood, becomes fragmented, weak, and confused. People begin to drop by the wayside. Recently when I met some leaders of a church, I told them that they had to have a presbytery to help them. Further, I told them that the worst thing they could do was to bring problems into the body where there were new believers. I told them that that would cause confusion for new babes in Christ. This is what they were doing. Can you imagine a household with five or six little children with mother and daddy having a disagreement and then bringing the children together for a meeting. Suppose at the meeting the parents say, "Now children, we are going to give to you our points of view and each of you must take sides." Oftentimes that is what happens in churches. And so they become fragmented.

We have examples in the Bible of this patrea

(fatherhood). The first example that we have of God moving to form a patrea among men is that of father Abraham. Genesis 17:1 says, "Now when Abram was ninety-nine years old, the Lord appeared to Abram and said to him, 'I am God Almighty, walk before Me and be blameless and I will establish My covenant between Me and you.'" You don't have to get discouraged if you haven't come into your fatherhood. Are you ninety-nine years of age? Father Abraham is given to us as an example, coming into his fatherhood at age ninety-nine. God said, "I will establish my covenant between me and you and I will multiply you exceedingly." Abram fell on his face and then God went on, saying, "As for Me, behold My covenant is with you. You shall be the father of a multitude of nations. No longer shall your name be called Abram but your name shall be called Abraham for I will make you a father of a multitude of nations. I will make you exceedingly fruitful and I will make nations of you and kings shall come forth from you. I will establish My covenant between Me and you and your descendants after you throughout their generations for an everlasting covenant to be God to you and to your descendants after you and I will give to you and your descendants after you the land of your sojournings, all the land of Canaan for an everlasting possession and I will be their God."

The name "Abraham" means literally, "the father of a multitude". God, in giving him the name Abraham, took first his name Abram which means "father" and then took a portion of His own name, the guttural sound of one of the names of God, and fused them together-----Abraham. In so doing, He then made Abraham the father over others. Abraham had the nature of Father God within him. He had the ability to bring forth. The only reason he was not a father was because his wife had been barren. But he had that nature to bring forth. He had the characteristic within him to be a natural father. But when God joined Himself to Abraham in covenant, Abraham became father of a multitude. That is, father in a fatherhood. He moved into a fatherhood and began to express the fatherhood of God. In Genesis 15:8, in order to accomplish this, God required Abram to cut covenant with Him. So He has Abram slay animals and lay the animals out, half on one side and half on the other. The blood flowed between the two halves. Then God put Abram into a deep sleep. While he was resting before the Lord, the Lord came as a flaming torch and walked between the two halves. God Himself walked between the two halves and by walking through the blood, declared that He would lay His own life down before He would break covenant with Abraham.

It is on this same basis that you and I come into our fatherhood within the multitude, the fatherhood within the family of God. After this occurred, God required Abram to cut covenant and declared that covenant in Genesis 17:10. He said, "This is My covenant, which you shall keep between Me and you and your descendants after you: every male among you shall be circumcised." Now this circumcision was the removal of a portion of the flesh of the body of every male. And the removal of the flesh had to take place at a certain place. It would have been much more convenient for God to say, "Why don't you just cut your hand and we will take some of the blood of the animal that we have slain and join it together with your blood because when the animal died, he died in God's place and in Abram's place. In the New Covenant that we have with God, Jesus died. But in the Old Covenant, the animal died on behalf of God and man. In the New Covenant, Jesus died on behalf of God and man and completed the promise that God gave to Abraham. But it would have been much more convenient for God to say, "You cut your hand and shed some of your blood and we will take some of the blood of the animal and we will mix them together and we will make covenant together. But God did not do it. He required Abram to go to that part of his body that made him an actual father, that allowed him to procreate, that allowed him to bring forth life. He had to have the circumcision, the removal of the flesh, declaring that his fatherhood is established in covenant. On the basis of that covenant he was established in his fatherhood. When Abram cut covenant with God through circumcision, God cut covenant with him through the slaying of the animals and they were joined as one. Then Abram became Abraham, the father of a multitude. In like manner, when our flesh is removed through the circumcision of Christ, we are freed from our selfishness and our self-centeredness and move into the pilgrimage leading up to our fatherhood. But if we do not move into our fatherhood, we remain child-like and self-centered. We would become disturbed if our children never grew up and never changed. God in like manner, becomes concerned if we do not change and grow up.

Our goal is to achieve fatherhood, coming to the place where we can assume responsibility for the formation of character in other people inasmuch as we have successfully transitioned through those stages. We have intentionally gone back to where, through confrontational relationships, husbandship reveals our weaknesses, and then have gone back to strengthen our weak foundations and to build again. That is the new birth process. It is God giving us a second chance, to be born again and made whole in Jesus Christ. I find in my own life that I could be moving along pretty well in some area in fatherhood and then discover a new area where I am acting like a child. The only thing that I can do if I want to change is to be willing to go back and deal with that weak foundation in my childhood and be made whole.

The first time I ever looked at these concepts, I thought that we needed a model of fatherhood and I did not know who that model could be. I had a mature father, a loving father. I remember him holding me many times in his lap and loving me. I remember wrestling with him. He would get down on the floor with me and would beard me and I would kick my feet and scream all the while asking him to do it again. We had a good time together. He also spanked and disciplined me. I could also point out some weaknesses in my father. As I grew older, I recognized that he had weaknesses in his life but at the same time he was a good father. Yet I could not use him as a model because he was not the perfect father. Then one day it dawned on me that we have a model of the Father and the Son in the scripture. It is Father God and the Lord Jesus. For God sent His son. In John 5 we find some evidence of what that relationship is like and what it was like when Jesus lived here physically and in the flesh as the Son of God. In John 5:19 Jesus begins revealing to us something of the relationship between Him and His Father God. In verse 19 he says, "Truly, truly I say to you that the Son can do nothing of Himself unless it is something he sees the Father doing." He says that whatever the Father does, these things the son also does in like manner. We could say it this way: The Father sets the pattern for the Son. As a Son, Jesus said, "I do what I see my Father doing and I do it like my Father does."

Now if we have had the opportunity to be raised in a christian home with a mature father, then it is easy for us to follow the pattern of fatherhood and then move into the pattern of Father God, because the first understanding that any human being has of

Father God, is his or her natural father. What if we did not have the opportunity to be raised by a mature father? In some cases, people are raised in the home of a father who has never worked through his own problems. So his child-likeness expresses itself in anger, resentment, fear, or an array of other serious problems. In other cases, the father was never present. I have talked to people who never knew a natural father. The father may have died before the child was born or before the child was aware of the presence of a father. I knew a young man who had been raised at stages by five different men. In each case, the son had to relate to a different man in his life. All of us need to understand that regardless of where we begin, whether in a healthy father relationship or a relationship where there was no father, or from being raised by an immature father, God gives us the opportunity to start over. That is the nature of the new birth-----being born again. Coming to the place where you can start over and can be born as a child of God, enjoying your childhood for a season. Just be as passionate about God as you care to be, to run around telling everyone that God does anything you ask of Him. We all want to go back and enjoy that.

Sometimes a person will say, "I don't know what has happened. There is something wrong with me. God used to answer every prayer of mine but He does not do it anymore." You want to say to them, "It is because He now has taken the bottle away from you. You are now supposed to be giving instead of receiving. You now have come to the place where you can impart. Just as Peter, in Acts, said, 'Silver and gold have I none but such as I have give I to thee.'" You begin to give to other people. A child receives by begging and asking. He goes around saying, "My Father loves me. I know because every time I ask, He gives to me." In Galatians 4 Paul says that as long as the heir is a child, he is a slave. He says that he is under guardians and managers. In verse 4, he says, "But when the fullness of time came, God sent forth His Son, born of a woman, born under the law in order that He might redeem those who are under the law that we might receive the adoption as sons." We move out of our childhood into our sonship. He says, "Because you are sons, God has sent forth the Spirit of His Son into our hearts crying, 'Abba Father.'" He sets us on course to move into that relationship to where we come to know Father. When we know Him, we turn to the multitude and begin to relate as Father relates because we have been with Father. That is His goal. This is the pattern that Jesus gave. Remember that in John, Jesus said, "Everything that the Father does, I do the same way." That is what we are after in teaching fatherhood within the church. Mature fatherhood is bringing a man or woman to the place where they know Father God and do what He does and say what He says.

When you get a group of leaders together who are fathers, they are committed only to doing what

Father does. If they are children and you bring them together and make them leaders, one of them will say, "I think we ought to do this," and another will say, "I think we ought to do that." Then they separate into opposite groups fighting each other. That is why the church is so fragmented.

Secondly, in John 5:20, Jesus says, "The Father loves the Son." So another pattern of fatherhood is that the father has the ability to express love in the son. First John points out that this is important to our lives. If you say that you love God and that you know God and you have this father relationship but you cannot love your neighbor, then the love of God is not in you. The love of God has equipped you to love the unlovely. The nature of fatherhood is that you love, not on the basis of that which is attractive to you, but on the basis of that which is needed. So you love the unlovely. You are able to bless. In John 3:35 Jesus said, "The Father loves the Son and has given all things into His hand." So the second characteristic of the Fatherhood of God is that He loves. The third is found in the first half of John 5:20 where Jesus says, "For the Father loves the Son, and shows Him all things that He Himself is doing." So it is the nature of the father to teach the son. God commanded Moses that the fathers would teach the children when they rise in the morning, when they walk by the way and when they lie down at night. (Deut 6:7)

If I could go back and raise our children again, I am certain that one thing I would do more of is devote more personal time to teaching my children when they were small. When they were older, I began to understand this. I started having classes with them personally and I believe it helped, but I missed some wonderful opportunities when their spirits were tender and very young, perhaps two through seven years of age. I missed those opportunities. The father teaches the son. He shows him what to do, not only by word, but by example. He teaches his son all things that he himself is doing and greater works than these will he show him that you may marvel.

The next characteristic of fatherhood is that the father brings the children to the place where they excel above the father. Is that the nature of Jesus? Jesus said, "These things that I do you shall do also and greater things than these shall you do because I go to the father." In other words, I am passing this nature of Father on to you. You are going to achieve far greater things than I have upon this earth.

Well, that is true. Through fatherhood within the church, there has been a broadening of the mission of the Father and the world has been reached more with the gospel because Jesus went to the Father and poured out His Spirit upon us that fathers might be established. Further in verse 22, He says, "For not even the Father judges anyone, but He has given all judgment to the Son." We might say it this way: The father delegates authority to the son. Jesus, in His fatherhood, said, "All authority is given to me in heaven and earth, go ye therefore and make disciples." I pass this authority onto you. Jesus trained His disciples in His fatherhood and taught them how to carry on His work. So He established the church through the multiplication of Himself into the lives of His disciples. That is the nature of fatherhood. I tell pastors that if the Lord were sending me out to start over again elsewhere and I had to start off with a new group of men, I believe the most effective thing that I could do is devote myself to working with those men to teach them these biblical principles. Then in verse 22, he says, "For not even the Father judges anyone, but He has given all judgment to the Son, in order that all may honor the Son even as they honor the Father." So the Father then honors the Son. We know that the Son honors the Father but the text here tells us that the Father also honors the Son.

I find sometimes that adults have a tendency to look upon children as something less than whole persons, but they are whole persons. They are complete and are to be honored and respected. One of the great sins of America today is the disrespect for childhood. Our nation has lost its fatherhood. We have very few fathers left anymore in our nation. Our fatherhood has been sacrificed on the altar of self-indulgence and we have missed what God has for us. The extreme of that is the killing of babies through abortion.

In verse 30 of John 5, Jesus says, "I can do nothing on My own initiative. As I hear, I judge; and My judgment is just, because I do not seek My own will but the will of Him who sent Me." The fatherhood of God was such that Jesus could willingly work under His authority and state that He did nothing on his own initiative but that He acted by what He was told to do. So He worked under that authority and did the will of His Father. In John 6:38, Jesus said, "For I have come down from heaven, not to do my own will, but the will of Him who sent Me. This is the will of Him who sent Me, that of all that He has given Me, I lose nothing." So Jesus made it clear that He could yield Himself to the will of the Father and that He could obey the Father in all things. In that type of sonship where we obey Father God, Father then can entrust to us His kingdom. This is what Jesus indicates in Luke 22:29 where He says, "and just as my Father has granted Me a kingdom, I grant you that you may eat and drink at My table in My kingdom, and you will sit on thrones judging the twelve tribes of Israel." When Jesus said, "Just as my Father has granted to me," the word "granted" in the original language derives its meaning from the root of the word "covenant". So Jesus speaks of the word "grant" in the sense of passing on through covenant. "Just as my Father has willed to me or left to me by nature of covenant a kingdom so I pass on to you the kingdom." So the Father grants the kingdom to the Son.

It is on the basis of this covenant and the granting that you are able to cast out demons, to heal the sick, to feed the poor, to see the multiplication of your bread. When you move into your sonship and into your husbandship and fatherhood, you see greater miracles take place. A child sees personal miracles. But a son, husband, and father see much greater miracles because it is there that you see the multiplication of your bread to feed the multitude. In John 10:15, Jesus makes the most important statement of all concerning the attitude between Father and Son when He says, "Even as the Father knows Me and I know the Father and I lay down My life for the sheep."

What you must understand here is that Jesus said, "The Father knows Me and I know the Father." The nature of Fatherhood is that we know our children. We know their spirit. We know what they need. Jesus said "the Father knows me." It is a relationship. It is not just knowing by name. It is a relationship to where you really know. So He said, "The Father knows Me and I know the Father." This is the foundation for a healthy relationship. This is our goal and we should all reach out for it and should not be afraid to recognize those areas in our life that still have resistance to the move of the Holy Spirit in bringing us into our fatherhood within the family of God. As Paul said, "I bow my knees to the Father in heaven from whom all fatherhood proceeds within the body of Christ." So we need to set this as a goal and honestly deal with those areas in our lives that are not yielding to the Holy Spirit. Because as we have seen in Galatians 4, when the Holy Spirit begins to move in our lives, when we are baptized in the Holy Spirit and His life is released through us, He will immediately begin trying to bring us into the fatherhood of the family of God. Much of the stress in our Christian life results from our resistance to Him, failing to yield to Him. It should be our attitude toward God that we can successfully make these changes and transitions by His grace at work in us.

Here are what I believe to be some important attitudes that will help to ensure your successful transition. In John 15:4, Jesus said, "Abide in Me and I in you. As the branch cannot bear fruit of itself unless it abides in the vine, so neither can you unless you abide in Me." Back in the mid 70's, there was a movement within the Body of Christ that was called Discipleship from which was born an idea relating to a natural tree. A natural tree has a big trunk and then primary branches from which spring secondary branches. As the idea goes, just as life flows from the trunk, up through the primary branches and finally to the secondary branches, so the life that flows through the body of Christ comes from Jesus, through principled leaders in the body of Christ and then from them out to the body.

I heard this theory and knew it was biblically in error. The problem was in the analogy. The tree of life is an unusual tree. It has a trunk and that trunk is Jesus who is rooted in the Father. And the only things springing from the trunk are the principle branches. Each one of us is a principle branch, a priest, and we are all connected to Jesus. We are connected to the trunk so that no human being can give you your life flow. All one can do is encourage and bless you, but you must be abiding in Christ. My wife abides in Christ. My children must abide in Christ and my fatherhood is that of bringing the family to the place where they abide in Christ, not that they abide in me and I in Christ. No, everyone is connected directly to Christ. Jesus said, "I am the vine and you are the branches."

Now, the teaching said, "I abide in Christ, my disciples abide in me, then they make disciples and those disciples abide in them." That is the teaching of Mormonism. Mormonism was founded upon a principle that the followers were connected to the leaders, Joseph Smith and Brigham Young and others. The key leaders of Mormonism said, "These are my followers and they will be joined to me for eternity and I hear from God and I get the flow from God and they get the flow from me." So to emphasize their point, they changed their last names. They said that their followers would be tied to them for eternity.

Sometimes we do the same thing. We say, "Oh, but we would not do anything like that." But you are doing just that if you are not abiding in Christ, if you are saying, "I cannot hear from God, I cannot really get the life flow unless I get it from someone else. You see, if you are not in the Word, if you are not abiding in Christ and the only source you have with God is some teacher telling you what God is saying, then basically, you are in the same danger area because you are not tied into Christ at all. The tree of life is a tree in which every branch goes straight into the trunk with no auxiliary branches at all. It is an unusual looking tree. You cannot draw a tree of life and have branches springing off branches. It just would not be scriptural. Jesus said that we must abide. It is in the abiding in the trunk, in the abiding in Christ, that you will begin to receive the life flow and start changing. The Holy Spirit will change you. You will begin to develop into your proper place within the family of God. Now, through this abiding, as stated in John 15: 7, you will become like Him: "If you abide in Me and my words abide in you, ask whatever you wish and it shall be done for you." You will begin to be more like Him. You will have that life flow.

Thirdly, in verse 10, through this abiding, you will find yourself obeying: "If you keep my commandments, you will abide in my love just as I have kept my Father's commandments and abide in His love." In other words, if you are abiding, you will keep the commandments, because it is in the abiding that you find the ability to obey the Lord, to keep His commandments. As you walk in obedience, you will find that obedience is much better than sacrifice in the eyes of God and God will be able to elevate you, to bring you to the place where He wants you to be. Then finally, beginning in verse 18, you will find that you will be able to endure hardship without letting it bother or hurt you: "If the world hates you, you know that it has hated Me before it hated you. If you are of the world, the world would love its own but because you are not of the world but I chose you out of the world, therefore the world hates you. Remember the word that I said to you, a slave is not greater than his master. If they persecuted Me, they will also persecute you. If you keep My word, they will keep yours, also. But all these things they will do to you for My name's sake, because they do not know the one who sent Me." Jesus makes it clear in this passage that we are to understand what it is that we are about in the Kingdom of God. We are not of this world. We do not have the nature of the world and the world is uncomfortable with us. They do not enjoy being around us because we do not think the way they think. We do not act the way they act.

Can you imagine how Jesus would act if He returned to the earth physically now as He did the first time. If He were to come, He would be unorthodox in so many ways because He would not be expressing the nature of the world but would be expressing the will of the Father. In like manner, when we begin to take on characteristics of Father God, we find ourselves behaving and living in ways that sometimes intimidate the world around us. That is okay. We just need to accept that as a part of the nature of being sons and daughters of God and that God will work in our lives. If we are not ready for that, then we will be threatened by those who want to reject us. There is always someone who will reject you. It is the nature of children to want approval and acceptance from those around them. The nature of the son is that we only want the acceptance of the Father. That's all! His approval is all we need.

Then we find ourselves moving in the authority of the Father and the world sees our authority and understands that we do have authority and that we are different. The world won't like it, but that is okay. You just rejoice in the Father and let Father bless you. This is certainly our goal. I know I have not achieved it yet, but I want to always be working toward it. I want to be open so that every time the Holy Spirit prompts me about areas in my life He wants to deal with, that I recognize it and move with Him. He can have the freedom and liberty to change me anytime and anywhere. Isn't that what you want, to be so open to the Lord that He has the liberty to change you, and free you from child-likeness, bringing you into mature fatherhood.

Can you say to the Father that you are open and willing to do the will of God? If you are willing to do His will, Jesus said in John, "You shall know what is of the Father." Commit yourself by saying, "I am willing to do your will Father. I am willing to be changed. I am willing to be totally subservient to You. I am open to You, Lord, with my life, my time, my relationships, my money, everything! I am open to You! My life is Yours!" That is what He is after, where you can come to the place where you can say,

"I do not act on my own initiative but whatever I see Father God doing, that I do in like manner."

Take on the gentle loving nature of Jesus and become fathers in the faith.

ABOUT THE AUTHORS

Bill Ligon holds a B.A. degree from Carson Newman College in Jefferson City, Tennessee; and the Master of Divinity from the Southern Baptist Theological Seminary in Louisville, Kentucky. He experienced the call of God on his life at age 18 and has ministered as a pastor-teacher since 1955. After serving student-pastorates in Tennessee and Kentucky while in school, he became the Assistant Pastor of the First Baptist Church of Tallahassee, Florida. He also served as pastor of the First Baptist Church in Madison, Florida; the Lee Street Baptist Church of Valdosta, Georgia; and the First Baptist Church of Brunswick, Georgia. He and his wife, the former Dorothy Jean Reeves of Tallahassee, Florida, served for six years as Southern Baptist Missionaries in Spain. The year 1970-71, Mr. Ligon was professor of Christian Ethics at Spanish Baptist Seminary in Barcelona, Spain, during which time he was baptized in the Holy Spirit. He founded Christian Renewal Church of Brunswick, Georgia in 1973, and served as Senior Pastor of the church since then. He is the author of the book, Discipleship: the Jesus View, published by Logos International and Imparting the Blessing.

John graduated from Oral Roberts University with a B.S. in Accounting. He serves as administrator of the ministry and has written a series of Children's Books on the Ten Commandments.

Web: thefathersblessing.com or 912-267-9140
Prices are subject to change

Imparting the Blessing
Pastor Bill Ligon has written a **book** showing the biblical principles on how to release the favor of God on you and your family. God reveals His heart to bless His people. See the redemptive power of the blessing. Learn to defend against the verbal curse. Plug into God's uplifting plan of blessing. $9.95

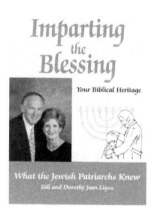

Blessing CD Album
The 4 CD Album of biblical principles on how to release the favor of God on you and your family. God reveals His heart to bless His people. See the redemptive power of the blessing. Learn to defend against the verbal curse. Plug into God's uplifting plan of blessing. $29.95

Web: thefathersblessing.com or 912-267-9140
Prices are subject to change

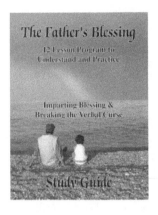

Blessing Study Program
A 12 Lesson program for a home or group study.
Leaders: $49.95
receive a 12 lesson study guide and 4 DVD album. The DVD's have Pastor Ligon introducing and discussing each lesson.
Students
receive a study guide $12.95

Practice the principles with weekly assignments.

Plan a special blessing service for your family.

Steps to Maturity
4 CD Album $19.95
The bible indicates four stages of spiritual growth that move a person from childish ways to maturity in Christ. Learn how to be brought to a responsible behavior and become a father in the faith. This series compliments the blessing materials.

Web: thefathersblessing.com or 912-267-9140
Prices are subject to change

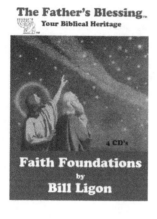

Faith Foundations

We please God by trusting Him and believing His word. All things are possible with God and in Christ Jesus all the promises of God are affirmed and freely given to us. We need therefore to understand the foundations of faith in order to engage God and His Kingdom fully by faith.
4 CD Album $19.95

Leadership Series

Pastor Ligon teaches the attitudes necessary to bring forth mature Christian leaders. Great insight for handling our modern day pressures. A insightful tool to help leaders in the church and home can act responsibly.
4 CD Album $19.95

Web: thefathersblessing.com or 912-267-9140
Prices are subject to change

The Anointing

The bible speaks of two anointings, one that fades and one that abides. Learn about the anointing that abides so that you too can develop an abiding relationship with the Holy Spirit.

4 CD Album $19.95

10 Commandments Children's Stories

God's Commandments are taught in the adventures of Sunny Valley. These stories are a great way to follow God's admonition to teach His Commandments to your children. Enjoy all 10 stories as the author tells these furry tales.

Audio CD $9.95

Web: thefathersblessing.com or 912-267-9140
Prices are subject to change

Beaver Sunday

One Sunday in Sunny Valley beavers are busy gathering wood for their home. If only they knew to honor the Sabbath, Benny Bee's home would not be in danger that day. What happens in this wonderful story leaves everyone smiling!
Hardback $9.95

Skippy and Miss June

June and Skippy are two happy bunnies that fall in love at a church picnic. They follow God's great wisdom and keep their love alive. They obey the 7th Commandment. Yea!
It's very sweet.
Hardback $9.95

The Bee and The Bear

Bobby Bear loves a fresh baked honey pie. Who can resist! He finds one that belongs to Benny Bee and soon learns the 8th Commandment, thou shall not steal.
Hardback $9.95

**Web: thefathersblessing.com or 912-267-9140
Prices are subject to change**

The One-O-Nine

It's a birthday party and a train story all wrapped up into one great adventure. Somewhere along the tracks Bobby Bear is tempted to lie. Oh me, oh my. Yet, once again God is watching out for him and shows Bobby Bear exactly what he really needs to do.

Hardback $9.95

The Father's Blessing Ministry is available to minister to you with a word of encouragement and prayer. If you would like to speak with us or have a prayer request sent to us please do so. Our mail address is PO Box 2480 Brunswick, GA 31523. Our web address is thefathersblessing.com and phone 912-267-9140. A form is available in the back of the book that you can tear out, send to us, and let us know your prayer need.

Please consider supporting the ministry through a onetime gift or becoming a monthly covenant partner that we might advance the Kingdom of God together and sow the gospel, truth, and faith into the hearts and lives of people where it is desperately needed.

Name:

Address:

City: **State:**   **Zip:**

Phone:

Email:

Prayer Request:

Please Contact Me: ☐

I would like to partner financially in this ministry:

One Time: ☐ $

Monthly: ☐ $

We would like to correspond with our partners by email with occasional newsletters.

e-mail address:

Phone:

If you are using a credit card:

Billing Name:

Billing Address:

Billing State: Zip:

Card Number:

Expiration: Security ID:

We always desire prayer for the ministry and ask that the Lord will always keep us in good health, will open affective doors of ministry, and that He will pour out His Spirit on all who are ministered to.

Mail To

The Father's Blessing
PO Box 2480
Brunswick, GA 31521

Phone: 912-267-9140
e-mail: contact@thefathersblessing.com